January

A Tanka Diary

M. Kei

Keibooks, Perryville, Maryland, USA, 2013

January, A Tanka Diary
Copyright 2013 by M. Kei
Cover photo courtesy of Berit <http://www.
flickr.com/people/9298216@N08> under a
Creative Commons Attribution 2.0 Generic license.

ISBN 978-0615871561 (Print)
Also available for Kindle.

Keibooks
P O Box 516
Perryville, MD 21903
Keibooks@gmail.com

Table of Contents

Author's Note

It is my custom to keep my journals in the form of short verse, principally tanka. In this manner I can record things of note, as well as observations of the world in a text-based series of snapshots.

Poetically speaking, many things happened in 2007, so I decided to set them down in the form of a book. It turned out to be a bigger undertaking than I expected, even though I left out all previously collected tanka appearing in *Heron Sea : Short Poems of the Chesapeake Bay* and *Slow Motion : The Log of a Chesapeake Bay Skipjack.* The former contains poems written before 2007, while the latter contains several hundred short poems, principally tanka, that were written while crewing aboard a workboat on the Chesapeake Bay. Taken together, *Slow Motion* and *January, A Tanka Diary*, give a complete account of published and previously unpublished tanka that I deem fit to print. (I have perpetrated just as many bad tanka as anyone else. Maybe more.)

Those who are familiar with my work will detect various sequences in their original, raw form, including *Asking Passage (Lynx), Autumn Water (3 Lights Gallery), The Bloody Veil (Red Lights), A Bridge of Bones (Lilliput Review), First Day of the Year (Modern English Tanka), The Heart of a Sailor, (World Class Poetry), Islands in the Chesapeake (Atlas Poetica), Legs of Invisible Desire (Atlas Poetica), Love Letters : Homoerotic Tanka of Love and Friendship (3 Lights Gallery), New Year's Dawn (Lynx), North of Superior (Atlas Poetica), Orion's Quiet (Simply Haiku), Remembering the Alamo (Simply Haiku), The Sailor's Ear (Bolts of Silk), Scattering Pearls (Skylark), Second Storm (Ribbons), Waterman's Spring (Lynx),* as well as many individual tanka.

~K~

January

January 1, New Year's Day

a fresh leaf
white in the winter
of a new year;
it seems a shame
to mar it with words

Donald Keene
shares my cup of tea
this new morning
  we talk about the death
  of tyrants and of poetry

raw and painful
this old blister;
if only our hurts
would change with
the calendar

M. Kei

    Muslim law:
a hanged body,
   neatly shrouded
will this small reverence
heal a bleeding country?

this journal,
bound in black,
a suitable coffin
for all the words
I have written

cold it is,
and colder still,
this dawn in
a new year
in an old house

in a few hours
I must face the sun—
without the grace
of age or humor,
but only memory

do they wake
to new hope
or old despair,
so many poor people
in this spinning world?

a worn threshold
between yesterday
and tomorrow,
no dawn
to light the step

as old as Janus,
these decisions between
past and future,
a threshold
where all men stumble

New Year's Day—
I wonder if
it is only the clouds
that make this day
so gloomy

M. Kei

I was silent
in the final days of the year,
but this dawn
offers new thoughts
about old worries

cricket,
why are you not here
singing the dawn
of a glorious
New Year?

it hardly seems
a new year,
no frogs chorus
its anthem,
no crickets sing its glory

cold,
these pearls of rain
strung in the needles
of a young loblolly
on New Year's Day

clay earth
won't hold the rain,
I try
to think of that when
drenched in worries

it's a day like any other,
full of melancholy
pessimism,
and yet—somewhere
there are herons

does the heron
bow his long neck
over the first fish
he has caught
this New Day?

New Year's Day
counting questions
in the lines of poems,
sometimes any syllables
are too many

M. Kei

a little ink
on my hand next
to the blister;
better to roll up the blind
and remember

  I heard them
last night, celebrating
   with fireworks
in this rainy dawn
I drink my tea alone

first cardinal
of the year,
on any day but this
your red would be
too red

dreams
and more dreams,
drenched
in the cold rain
of a new year

with great deliberation
I muse over my choices
but choose the same tea
I always choose—
the illusion of options

a creature of habit,
I begin this new day
the same as any other:
with words spilled in black
on a white winter day

new, this tea mug,
with clouds of milk
in a tannin sky,
but enough sugar
will sweeten this dawn

my tea mug
pictures a lighthouse
no longer standing;
do wives remember
better days?

M. Kei

no sun,
but still the day brightens,
a lesson, perhaps,
for one given to
poetry and fantasy

New Year's Day—
the one day
of the year
she might
remember me

now I have a reason
to keep watch at this window;
a hope that today of all days
she will remember me
with kindness

New Year's Day
once she was real, but
she has dwindled at last
to a memory and
scattered poems

these boys,
they say they like
my poems—
but they lie sleeping
in the damp dawn

another
sip of tea,
the seagull flies
to me
through the porcelain sky

she starts her year
like many others,
exhausted
alone
in despair

dishes, too,
waiting for
the cold dunk
of water
on New Year's Day

M. Kei

<u>January 2</u>

second day
of the new year,
do I have any
more hope today
than yesterday?

it's a grey night
that makes me long for
the blue-green moon
of summer storms
and tornado shelters

another afternoon
of empty mailboxes,
not even a pigeon
to write its message
in the sky

January 3

what spirit flew
out of this hole
in winter's snow?
on the other side
a flock of wild geese

her mouth—
his body shudders,
a tall tree feeling
the blows of the axe
that will topple it

winter night
  one candle in
    the evening light
his passion spent
  he flickers out

M. Kei

his hands claw the carpet,
  desperate
    for handholds
      to keep him from
  falling off the world

a sailor before
the tsunami,
he drowns in
the flood tide
of her desire

January 4

dawn on
another continent;
still this young man
keeps me company
tonight

there is nothing
quite so delightful
as someone
eager to learn
all my vices

so many windows
on yesterday,
but none
that see into
tomorrow

M. Kei

January 5

blue flag iris—
for so many years
I never knew your name,
yet, all these homes
you made for me

January 6

January heat wave
seventy degrees—
the creek bottoms
  full of fog &
    barefoot boys

different darks—
am I drawn
to you because
your despair is
not my own?

there are times
when I know
the secrets of the universe;
but never when
I am awake

M. Kei

in the end,
it comes down to
the inadequacy of poets
tiny blue flowers
unnoticed in the grass

when the world of men is gone,
who will scatter
the ashes of our existence,
who will place the memorial
of our dying?

hearing the ghosts of
Indians on his trail,
he looks back
I do not reassure him
with my smile

January 7

a warm winter:
God's mercy to the poor
I say my thanks
and ask
for yet more grace

Persian carpet,
my denim leg over
your bare one,
my book resting
against your back

it was a shock
to see his name again
and feel
my queerness awake
after silence

M. Kei

I miss the thrumming
of his great heart,
skin stretched tight
over a small frame
bursting with intelligence

sometimes
the only light in my life
comes from
opening the
refrigerator door

going to the funeral
it snows a little in Illinois;
coming home
from the funeral,
it snows a little in Illinois

January 11

a bit of green
in a sidewalk crack—
perhaps
i have already
been reincarnated

grandma's pewter—
we are not a family
to inherit silver
I flick the side and
it rings a little hollow

mother's favorite,
the Sleepy Eye pitcher,
crockery Indians
not yet gone extinct
in the antique shop

M. Kei

you can't run forever,
but there's no reason
not
to try and get
a good head start

January 14

he beats
the carousel pony
to make it run;
he's that
sort of man

his relatives don't like him,
so he tells them
he's sleeping with
a famous male poet
twice his age

his sleep-drowned baritone
rumbles beneath the covers,
a slight tremor
that might mean nothing
or everything

M. Kei

<u>January 20</u>

mourning dove
her head bobbing
at the window
examining the captive
within his cage

to others
it is a vacant lot,
but to me,
a new world full
of unexplored territory

the old blister
still hurts,
another new year
creeps in
on wounded feet

moving house,
I find her mother's
wedding dress—
eighteen years of memories,
I keep this too

hungry,
the poor man struggles
through the snow,
baby in his arms,
little girl in his footprints

a promise
of snow unfulfilled,
the moon shines
on this house,
this sleeping man

the vacant lot
full of discarded
Christmas trees—
my heart flutters with
the scraps of tinsel

M. Kei

a vacant lot
full of weeds
and mourning doves,
today my heart
is just like that

silver sun
in a winter sky,
how many dreams
will tarnish
before you set?

a cold winter night,
only Orion
for company
and this book of
someone else's poems

a house finch
in her red apron,
a titmouse
in his brown suit,
can spring be far away?

slate-backed junco,
herald of the winter snow,
how chill the day
with your grey wings
fluttering at my window

it's a heavy head
I hang over
this book of poetry,
wondering if the masters
might rub off on me

mid-winter
a single bamboo sprouts
in a vase;
my heart greens
at the thought of spring

a black cat
slips through the dusk;
I wish I had
paws
as soft as night

M. Kei

the entire sky
a threnody in grey,
a Whistler painting
without a sound,
not even birdsong

green enough
this winter grass
for sparrows
and lonelyhearts
to browse

a filthy rag
wraps my broken hand,
one more thing
to teach me patience
in this life

she loved
yellow roses
and white daisies,
my mother,
now deceased

there was a time
when all my thoughts
were brown
like the little birds
that flutter through winter

great storms
announce themselves
with small breezes;
I find your letter
in my mailbox

winter day—
the crispness of
the celery
as I prepare
to dine alone

you'd think
a poet would know
something about love
I sweep dusty webs
from all the corners

M. Kei

second hand
marching around
the dial,
why do you
shine so bright?

no consolation
in the violins tonight;
this too will pass
into dust and ashes
on a winter's day

so very tired,
but I don't want to sleep—
my days are too short
for dreams that
never come true

somewhere
beyond the streetlights,
there are stars
brighter than
any dream

visiting new people,
I discover a skipjack model
in their den
we settle in for hours
of sea yarns

no coat
in the winter wind
at the pay phone
I call home
collect

perhaps Bach
knew this night
would come—
he wrote these toccatas
just for me

i was born
under a faint star
and that has ruled
my fate in this
mortal world

M. Kei

it's a minor key,
this Scarlatti sonata,
but how the notes fly!
there is beauty
even in sadness

January 21

at the edge of the thicket,
four red cardinals
and one female,
pecking
at winter's leavings

it's because of January
that God made cardinals;
when our hearts are weary
of the long grey cold
and we yearn for spring

if it weren't for
the greenness of the weeds,
this vacant lot
would be a place
of devastation

M. Kei

I am fond of weeds,
hardy things that grow
and bloom,
no matter what
difficulties they face

the dawn has yet
to reach these earthly shadows,
but up there in the light
bay gulls zoom past
chasing the joy of day

   it's a day
unlike any other,
this bright dawn
full of cardinals
      and hope

often I encounter
women shivering outside,
talking to their
cell phones,
but never their men

a curmudgeon,
I suppose, this man
who sits
staring at winter weeds,
hoping for mourning doves

it's a winter day,
but the tides still
ebb and flow,
bay gulls still wing
through a silver sky

M. Kei

January 22

God's hand opens
and cardinals flutter forth—
proof that even
this winter grief
will pass

January 24

a raveled thread,
my life,
untwisting into
gossamers that
blow away

lately my t-shirts
have a theme:
sailing vessels
carried on my back
as they carried me

January 27

her screw
still turning as she
went down,
the *Sarah C. Conway*,
dead at 114

it hurts to know
so many bones of
dead vessels
lie in watery tombs
beneath my feet

all silted up,
the Elk River will
never know
another gull-winged
schooner

could there be
anything sadder to see
than an old schooner,
her sails wung out,
hogbacked and grey?

February

February 1

if only there were
mourning doves outside
my window,
i might feel the winter
understood my feelings

M. Kei

February 2

first birdsong of the year
somewhere,
amid all the brown gloom,
a small life is
happy to greet the day

February 7

there was a time
when I had faith in
a better future;
now it is enough to
breathe ordinary air

M. Kei

<u>February 8</u>

little junco
on wings of storm,
you never tire
of the winter
at your back

February 9

tanka and
wooden sailboats are
necessities of life;
without them, my heart
grows cramped and stale

M. Kei

February 10

it leaves
a taste
in my mouth,
this clipping
of student's wings

February
a day so cold,
for once I'm glad
I didn't have to sail
these bitter waters

I miss the boat
crave it
the water
the herons
and the world

February 12

drinking
in Jimmy Buffet's bar
on Saba,
I consider
the vagaries of fate

grey ghost
in the winter woods,
unlike you, tree,
I will not be born again
on a spring day

there aren't any
snow angels this winter,
no children in red caps
pretending that
God is real

M. Kei

raisins
boxed and labeled
their sweetness kept
for a later day—
the old woman nods

February
the furnace
rattles through the night,
never listening
to what winter says

some day
my ghost will be
hiroshimaed against these walls,
a silhouette of life
no longer lived

astrologer-poets
argue about stars,
Orion and his hounds
continue across
the winter sky

he is no Romeo
she is no Juliet
but they two will lie
in the brown earth
their stories red

the *Sarah C. Conway*
sinking through a hole
in the storm . . .
what spirits flew out
of this white world?

M. Kei

<u>February 25</u>

it was
the kind of moon
that called for
train whistles,
but gave only memories

a flight of hawks
lifting the clouds
with their wings,
winter settles heavier
without them

a morning
without sparrows,
just the debris
of a long winter
tapping the window

a few flakes
shaken out of
a salt cellar sky,
a little seasoning
for the pavement

white flakes falling,
Beethoven on the stereo,
a stray cat
skitters past
the glass door

on a winter morning,
small things take on
unusual importance:
hand lotion, toilet paper,
forgotten lovers . . .

in a winter moment,
snow falls
in a white veil,
'Für Elise'
plays on the stereo

M. Kei

distracted
only a moment by
the falling snow,
my son resumes
his videogame

March

March 4

the male catches the eye,
but looking closer,
three female cardinals
peck the seeds of winter
at the thicket's edge

M. Kei

<u>March 7</u>

snow mist
a brown cardinal
her red beak
carrying
spring's promise

snow mist
a faint dusting of white
spun sugar
on the hard realities
of rural poverty

Queen Cardinal
in your dowager weeds,
why do so many
brilliant males court you,
but never me?

64

today the red of cardinals
is too much to bear,
send me the sight
of dowagers
in their feathered weeds

snowy blue jay,
pecking at
the remnants of dawn,
searching for the summer
yet to be born

what is a man
but a worm clinging
to a plank,
lost in the immensity
of God's great ocean?

walk with me to some place
the lamplight doesn't reach
    in the darkness
share forbidden kisses
    the sun denies

M. Kei

March 15

a few dark figures
under a dagger moon
huddle together
beneath the overpass
and passing time

March 16

no respite from the rain,
even the cardinals look
a little bedraggled
the first day
of flood season

amid the dead weeds
and fallen branches,
her red beak
gives her away,
the cardinal's wife

no loblolly
at this window,
just the
toppled remains
of vine-killed trees

M. Kei

this rainy day,
she keeps company
with the little brown sparrows,
Mrs. Cardinal in her
widow's weeds

two red beaks!
somewhere,
in all that brown,
there must be
a pair of cardinals

today perhaps
I'll buy a little bird seed
so there is something
to find after all
that effort

after days
without sparrows,
suddenly a flood
of little brown birds
in the middle of the rain

are they warm
in their feather coats,
these little sparrows
flocking in the
cold, cold rain?

quiet now
sleet falling from
the grey sky
no bird flitting
through the trees

sudden sun—
the ice becomes
a sheet of diamonds
too dazzling for
the heart

M. Kei

March 18

North East, Maryland,
a vein of blue smoke
against the winter sky,
an old black man
huddles over his cigarette

crawling into the bilge,
the wood still damp even
in the middle of winter,
the cold wind blowing
through her seams

Sabbath
is given to the boat,
God's work,
sustaining something that
matters more than me

jamming my chest
against the stringer,
I realize why women
don't like this
kind of work

winter maintenance
two hours after
I crawl out of the bilge
of an old boat,
my butt's still cold

the sky
so blue today,
if only my heart
might change
like the weather

M. Kei

March 24

yesterday
the river bottom
was a bowl of fog,
today,
the first green buds

tails twitching,
white-throated sparrows
forage
the wet green grass
of spring

leaning on
the window sill,
my daughter
helps me count
white-throated sparrows

mudstained
boots and jeans
a pocket full of birds
a grey spring day
with wings like mallards

M. Kei

<u>March 25</u>

perched on a
bare branch,
the cooperhawk
watches the tourists
who never notice

a fine spring day—
mallards in combat
for the favor of a hen,
the lagoon roiled by
feathers and beaks

March 28

twilight maryland,
acres of seagulls
in the fields . . .
they named this road
"Gold Star Mother Highway"

March 30

Rodgers Tavern—
everything derelict
stone, history, ferry,
yet George Washington
slept here

crows and
train trestles,
the only company
at the crest
of Perry Point

the road passes
the old stone tavern and
green lawns,
leaving behind history
and a rusty train trestle

pungy pink
and river red,
a tugboat
tied to the shore
waiting for work

no green in
the spring marsh,
a tangled thicket
of brown sleeping
beneath a barren sun

at Rodgers Tavern,
a single sparrow
chirps and whistles,
calling
the warm sun of spring

a broken fence,
half dead yews,
and moss,
but the jonquils
bloom yellow

M. Kei

outside
the broken fence,
the world
shifts to something
a little wilder

the motorcycle riders
didn't stay long,
a cigarette or two
and they were
gone again

Perry Point:
one faded
American flag
stands guard over
Pvt. Jackson's grave

mackerel sky
and a dormant marsh,
cut by a rusty
train trestle over
a brown river

not quite straight
the path from
the old tavern
to the ferry landing
after all these years

the color of hope—
pink magnolia trees
blooming
against the windows
of the veterans hospital

the sign says,
"in loving memory"
but
the tree is dead
its trunk shattered

M. Kei

Chesapeake night
in the middle of it,
one skipjack,
moths fluttering
around her masthead light

April

April 1

a book of poetry later,
my hands still
smell like this afternoon's
Copperkote and
the bilge of an old boat

my son and I
crawl through the bilge
of an old wooden boat,
painting Copperkote
for another fifty years

ladled out of
mother's womb,
I continue to
splatter and spill
this life of mine

M. Kei

<u>April 6</u>

scooting in the sawdust
beneath the boat,
my son holds the flashlight
while I tar the inside
of the centerboard well

sitting on a stack of lumber,
my daughter strips the paint
from a piece of
metal hardware
to be restored to the boat

anointed
with tar after working
on the boat,
I take a bath in WD-40
and come out slick and clean

April 7

one spot of tar
I didn't remove—
a tattoo of
winter work
upon my skin

it's a place
like no other,
full of the ghosts
of wooden boats
and dying men

neither Homer
nor Alanis Morissette
saw this amber moon
lustrous in the waters
of the Chesapeake

M. Kei

once more
a noon of feathered joy,
small birds
singing the anthem
of spring newly born

April 8

mostly dead,
but still a few branches
send out
green leaves
this chilly day

being a poet,
I can only speak to you
through a mask
that looks like
my own face

M. Kei

<u>April 9</u>

me and my limp
thumping along
the promenade
as pretty girls
rollerskate past

April 10

another reluctant day
torn from this chair,
this window,
not even a sparrow
to miss my going

tempted to play hooky
but I have students waiting,
    this day without a morning
    this night without a day
in the shadow of a sparrow

did I expect
enlightenment?
    this open window
    this open mind
this blank page

M. Kei

there was
a day when I thought
I was a god . . .
bird seed scattered
uneaten on the ground

so many crosses
on the side of the road,
my student tells me
which one was
his best friend

April 12

brushing my teeth,
I pause to listen—
my daughter's singing
drifts down the hall
through the closed door

Diet Barq's Rootbeer—
she is particular
about these things,
my daughter who is now
the woman of the house

M. Kei

April 13

where are they,
all the little birds
who used to
gladden my
winter mornings?

promises I make:
to help my daughter
sew her dress
so that she can dance
the dream she almost forgot

April 15

another
book of tanka
for review—
sparrows chirping
in the spring rain

the green tide of spring
slowly seeps across
the vacant lot,
a discarded book
beside an open blind

the nightlight flickers,
uncertain if
it is day or night;
I feel much the same
about my growing daughter

M. Kei

sheets of rain—
nowhere can I see
the sparrows,
but still the brightness
of their small voices

a little snow
mixed with the rain,
and a robin
perched on his
eternal limb

three dollars
to live on
until Friday
slips in
through the keyhole

April 16

in the mud
next to the asphalt,
a broken doll's head,
a crow pecking
at plastic eyes

derelict memory,
a broken watch washed up
on a muddy beach
next to the orange foot
of a Canada goose

walking the street
with legs of invisible desire,
looking in windows
at the people for sale
but I have no money

M. Kei

without an audience,
the poet's heart has no meter,
ears give voice
to the red paper
brushing along the ground

in the used book store,
the shopkeeper tells me,
"Poetry doesn't sell."
I buy a book I don't want
to prove him wrong

April 17

months later,
a broken string
of Mardi Gras beads,
gold stars crushed
into the carpet

a tree full
of blackbirds
taking off one by one,
like fighters from
an aircraft carrier

this green cove
where I return after
long days at sea
is the only place
I wish to drop my anchor

M. Kei

April 18

married
to the tune of 'Greensleeves,'
now divorced,
"Alas my love,
you do me wrong."

April 19

in a room
with no wind,
a flickering candle
  is that you,
   mother?

some mornings
when the sky
is still grey
a cat with amber eyes
walks through my dreams

it is difficult
to get the news from poems,
but every day
men kill for the lack
of what is found there

M. Kei

April 20

saltwater
drying on my back,
sun slipping
into the shadowed place
you will not follow

April 21

what lesson
was I supposed to learn?
staring at white heroes
surrounded by the walls
of the Alamo

This is the room
where Davy Crockett died.
   later,
   my mother
   eating jalapeños

thirty-five years
since the dust of Texas
stained my boots,
I wonder if I can
find the family graves

M. Kei

the captain's mess—
politely
telling his
drunk fiancée
"no"

white orchids
on a black Hawaiian shirt,
rum
on the deck behind
the captain's house

cargo shorts,
what dreams
will I stuff
into these pockets
today?

feeling hungover
after only one drink,
the bitter taste
of a party where
I am a stranger

my daughter
singing in the dark
for an audience
of bats
and a single dog

a thin white crust
of moon
scattered in
a blue sky,
a perplexing party invite

April 22

Joshua Bell
busking in the Metro,
the sounds of the Stradivarius
pure and clear
above the rush hour rustle

white-throated sparrow,
do you recognize
the sounds
coming from
the Stradivarius?

how very white
the crown of this
little sparrow
as Joshua Bell
plays in the background

people rushing
to and fro,
something has to
occupy their minds,
but what?

not fond of crab,
but don't tell,
or they'll
run me out
of Maryland

April 23

rite of passage:
I donate my old wheelchair
to the museum
why am I tempted to
borrow it back?

one hundred tanka . . .
surely all these words
must mean something
outside,
more brown birds

they go back
where they came from,
these great brown birds,
but I have no desire
to travel with them

one bamboo
in a vase full
of pebbles,
holding winter
at bay

ten years
since she married
someone else;
why does it bother me
to forget her birthday?

math major—
she guesses the
correct number
of gummi worms
in the jar

M. Kei

<u>April 24</u>

if only
this clock would melt,
thaw, and resolve itself into a dew,
and set me free
like a Salvador Dalí painting

limousine moment:
the grease monkey
holds open
the door to
my beater

April 27

homesick
I discover
the beauty of
a snake garden
in the April rain

a robin's
shiny black head
in the rain,
Mussorgsky
on the stereo

May

May 2

I should resent
getting kicked out of
the Student Union,
but the carillon
chimes May vespers

the pudgy
security guard did
me a favor
kicking me out
into a May evening

alone in this
green evening,
nothing but
iris leaves
for company

M. Kei

every one
walks past azalea buds
on the way to
the parking lot
and the trip home

under the
flowering dogwood,
even the rattle of
the rubbish cart
is a kind of music

a student
in a white shirt and
blue tie,
doesn't he know this night
will never come again?

"Library"
says the sign,
but who stops
to read the
Book of the World?

I wonder if
they are as bored
as I am,
those students whose
class I overhear

only in spring
is the crabtree admired,
but this root
marks the
goldfish's grave

my sister must have
lilies-of-the-valley
two years after
  her mother dead
  her son dead

khakis,
name tag and glasses—
I could be mistaken
for the professor
I am not

M. Kei

in the college corridor,
the faint ululation of
an Arabic prayer
  which mirror
  are the students looking into?

overhead
a hawk with a snake
in its beak—
suddenly I
think of Mexico

May 3

this scarred finger
never hurt me all these years,
why now, when
I am not ready to grow old
does it begin to pain me?

once again
feeling the arthritic
knuckle,
pretending not to notice
wrinkles in my hands

the fire alarm!
suddenly the prospect
of eventual
old age and death
no longer seems important

M. Kei

internal shore
a little haze
lingering
between here
and there

May 6

trash tells me
that other feet have
trod this trail,
but today
I am the first

windchimes—
tall saplings
bare of leaves
sway and rattle
their branches

the flash of
a cottontail
tells me
these boots
are too loud

M. Kei

a moss carpet,
greening before
the trees
acquire new leaves
and close the forest room

two dark birds
hopping through
the underbrush,
slated-colored, like storms
without names

little birds,
red as a hawk's tail
but small
as a sparrow,
flicker and are gone

the cool of the woods
gives way to field sun,
acres of briar roses
and bumblebees
yet to bloom

last year's
brown weeds
slowly sink beneath
a rising tide
of new green

warm sun
gives way to
cool green shadows—
the path less traveled
has made all the difference

"nothing in haste"
the brambles remind me,
gently, slowly,
ease through
the difficult parts

robins
the blackness of
their heads
proclaims
the mating season

M. Kei

outside the wall of green,
an unwelcome voice,
car horns, traffic,
the sound of my own feet,
and then the sighing of the wind

white blooms
of woodland strawberries
darkened for just a moment
by the flicker of
a bird's passing shadow

woodland hiking—
the earth still chill,
the youngest shades
of green being born,
heralded by the birds

shining like a mirror:
the end of a discarded
beer can
before the weeds
cover it

wooden debris
rusty nails
broken glass—
signs of intention
now abandoned

the plank remembers
the tree from which it came,
slowly dividing
along natural lines,
returning to the earth

try as I might,
I cannot help these boots
trammeling green things;
the cracking of sticks
rebukes my heavy ways

stones at the root
of tall trees
covered in moss;
the bones, sinew, and skin
of earth himself

M. Kei

something large
and not human
lay down in these weeds,
made a nest,
and rested a while

looking back,
the trail I have left
is ragged
and wandering,
a stranger to this land
.

a sunny thicket—
blinded,
I cannot find my way
in shadows
unless I too am shadow

the vines cover
the chainlink fence,
determined
that this too will return
from whence it came

that trail
through a tunnel
of greenery
wasn't made for
human beings

an orange stake
labeled "control point"
flagged with
blue and white ribbons
in the middle of the woods

discarded soda cans,
"Moon Mist" flavor
next to the stake
that calls itself
"control point"

again that
barking birdsong
I know so well,
but never have I seen
the one who sings it

M. Kei

walking through
tall weeds beside
the highway,
the white bones of
a deer skeleton

memento mori—
the white bones
of a deer
slowly sinking
into the loam

hollow ribs,
empty of marrow,
hollow vertebrae,
empty of will,
all things come to this

no skull nor pelvis,
but an empty soda bottle
where a heart should be,
the bones disturbed
before I ever found them

today
I take a path
never taken
that can never be
taken again

the remains
of another dead deer—
the stench drives me back
to view gnawed legbones
and a torn pelt

a nest of dead grass
where the doe first lay,
her legbones torn away
and licked clean by
something hungry

those first bones
were so very small—
without the dead doe
I would have never
known the fawn

M. Kei

a bramble rose
snags my sleeve—
a reminder of
this living world
about to bloom

five
creamy white petals
the first briar rose
blooms
beside my boot

a faint perfume
from a tree with
pale flowers,
this too is a thing for which
I have no name

dead deer
and white blooms—
this is a thing
I will not
soon forget

clumps of
yellow blooming weeds
in this field
it is I am who am
useless and unwanted

I want to go home now—
this forest no longer
gives me passage,
brambles and deadfalls
block my way

thorns grab
my clothes and
hold me back,
but a rock
offers me a place to rest

this cool breeze,
this bed of wild
strawberries in bloom,
bird calls all around,
perhaps I shouldn't leave

M. Kei

in these
freshly toppled weeds,
I recognize my own trail
and follow myself back
to whence I came

after the woods,
the bleeding hearts
planted by
a previous tenant
are pleasantly domestic

pale shoots
of pine candles on
the loblolly,
everything green
is born again

the tree
I thought was dead,
even it sends forth
yellow-green leaves
from all its slender branches

living in the rear apartment,
I am grateful for
the landlord's neglect
that permits
wild things to grow

my black boots
still in the shower,
drying off
after hiking
through the woods

M. Kei

May 10

Bridal Veil Falls—
I saw them as a child
two divorces later
they remain a vision
never quite forgotten

a slow train
north of Superior,
pausing
to pick up and drop off
Indians, milk, and skiers

a green valley
but my mother bleeding
red, red, so red
these are the secret things
a child never forgets

May 11

water world—
the tree of heaven
an island
in the middle
of the fog

mockingbirds
flirting and flitting
in the parking lot—
beige beauties
in the summer sun

M. Kei

May 12

blue flag iris,
a piece of driftwood,
a pebble beach,
these are the things
that stay a traveler's steps

May 14

lowest tide—
the pushboat's propellor
stirs a coffee cup
in the bottom of
the yacht basin

M. Kei

May 16

all afternoon
the threat of rain
grows heavier;
the sky settles on
unwilling shoulders

cantaloupe,
maraschino,
tangerine—
crayons good enough
to eat

a line of
lavender wisteria along
the highway;
for a moment I forget
his death

a male and
female cardinal
touch beaks
for just a moment
in the drizzling rain

squealing like
she just saw Elvis,
she tells me
she likes
my poems

an American flag
behind the captain
at the helm;
behind that
an even taller tall ship

golden breasts
polished by the sun,
barn swallows
swifter than thought
vanish in the skies

M. Kei

May 18

throwing away
old papers,
I found a love letter—
I vaguely recall
that boy-man

cleaning house,
I discover
an old diary
who did I
used to be?

last year it was
nothing but chokecherry
blooms for his grave;
this year wisteria
and a hesitant future

May 24

May,
the first wild rose
small white petals
light up the edge
of the forest

M. Kei

May 27

May evening
the chill humidity
a harbinger of summer
even the grackles
have lost their luster

May 28

racing a thunderstorm
back to port,
forty knots in my face
and one chance to
throw the bowline

M. Kei

May 29

a bit of glitter
stuck to the center
of her forehead:
her third eye
shining at the world

wood thrush
outside this prison window,
stay a bit longer
so that my soul
may know freedom

an elderly friend
slips into his dotage,
in the distance
a fast moving freight train
leaves this town behind

how am I
to know
what I am
without the mirror
of your disapproval?

"red, right, return"
the red light on
the nun buoy
a welcome sight
this hazy night

running against
the storm,
the red light of
the nun buoy
offers haven

orange lightning
in the distance,
the comfort of
the nun buoy's red light
guiding us to port

the old flat
faced east,
and so
I gloried
in the dawn

Grand Marnier ice cream—
the delightful discovery
that it is possible
to get drunk
on simple things

reading a book
of someone else's
love poems,
I sigh a little and
turn to the dawn

May 30

the world outside
full of the whirling news
of destruction,
but inside
this cup of tea

stepping out my door
into the green evening and
the perfume of wild vines,
   a world without shadows
   a world without fears

not quite the same,
a beige cardinal and
the ivory teapot,
each touched with
a brighter color

the cardinals' wives
are frequent guests
to my backyard,
their crowned heads
nodding agreement

sifting through
the window screen
this evening,
the yellow scent of
wild vines blooming

the round back
of a sleeping cat
arranges all
the angles to
a comfortable curve

a house
is never
a home
until the cat
moves in

ah, you Zen seeker!
let the cat
teach you
to let go
and let be

there is no need
to go to the mountain
in search of peace,
the cat is
right here

June

June 2

squirt guns
lying in the grass,
beside them
an empty bottle
of Hennessy

withered
on the vine,
the scent of
the last
honeysuckles

M. Kei

<u>June 3</u>

creeping jenny,
face pale in
the early morning,
turned up,
waiting for rain

brown thrasher
tilting your head
to study the sky,
what do you see
that I do not?

the trees
begin to talk,
tossing their green heads
and whispering
about the weather

sailor's ear—
I hear the trees
whispering
and feel the cold touch
of premonition

the wooden ketch
and the old schooner
know the winds
I watch them
watching the clouds

ashore,
Mardi Gras beads rattle
against the lamp
and remind me of
halyards in the storm

the tree
disappearing under
three kinds of
invasive vines—
I understand how it feels

cold on bare skin:
the summer breeze
whispering about
rain and wind
just over the horizon

honeysuckle
through the window—
I raise my head
in time to see
cardinals courting

all morning
a cool tease of drizzle,
just in time
for the boat to launch,
a downpour

my daughter
comes to my window
to call me out
barefoot
into the rain

creeping jennies
closed up in the cold rain,
I teach my daughter
the secrets of
wild things

the coldness
of the rain,
the thunder of
the freight train,
and the voice of Willie Nelson

a recruiter
for the corrections department:
petite, blonde, and ladylike,
she assures us that the jail
is clean and not too dark

tempted myself
to talk with some of
the employers
who are recruiting
my students

M. Kei

is it fear
or good sense
that keeps me
in a job
I don't like?

the ache of
my repaired teeth,
the ache of
my damaged
wallet

long shadows
in the morning dew
little birds
hopping in and out
of the light

tiny white wings
rise through
the dewy weeds
and vanish
in the dawn

<u>June 8</u>

days
unwinding into
months
unwinding into
death

M. Kei

<u>June 16</u>

a little ragged
(much like the inhabitants
of this apartment)
the bleeding heart
on the patio

June 22

how can we do
what we know
we should not?
a brown flood
roiling at the doorstep

M. Kei

June 23

waking
the same time
as always,
this first day of
being unemployed

June 24

thunder cracks—
at home,
our tempest
hardly rattles
the teapot

M. Kei

June 26

another skipjack
headed for the grave
the *Flora A. Price*
"friend ship of Caroline County"
begging for a home

June 29

mere air
this shimmering day
hovering
over shimmering water,
and yet . . .

a leaf
green and curled
drawn up yet limp
in the June drought
tense with waiting

afloat on
a rotten plank,
this man's heart
lost in the narrow sea
of the Chesapeake

M. Kei

the wave
always returns
to lap this strand
of broken stone
and empty dreams

one green finch
blown across
the asphalt
and into
the tree of heaven

double silver
rings around my
smallest finger,
dressing up
the arthritic knuckle

little enough rain,
but rain it is,
falling through
the long day of dreams
and into the night

you'd think
as old as I am,
this youth desiring me
would delight, but—
performance anxiety

the only man
in the Breast Health Center
contemplates
images of women
growing gracefully older

the only man
in the Breast Health Center
wonders if someday
his aging body will
be celebrated like these

Breast Health Center:
women on the walls,
in the brochures,
working the desk
out here, one man, waiting

M. Kei

how can the weeds
be so lush this rainy day?
I undergo testing
to see if my bones are
fragile like an old woman

something else
buds into bloom
I slide
the silver ring splint
off and on my hand

playing with
the ring splint,
watching it spin
and rattle,
a little like my mind

outside,
the birds chatter
about things
that matter
to birds

July

July 2

I didn't know
he was dying when
I stood on
the quarterdeck of his
soon-to-be widowed ship

pretty soon
I'll have to get up and
go back to work
another summer seeping
into the wood of the boat

another Sunday
spent worshipping in
the cathedral of the Chesapeake,
this wooden boat
the only pew

M. Kei

July 4

iris leaves
and a few golden
peaches
scattered on
the picnic blanket

July 5

robin
at the top of
the tree of heaven,
can you see
God from there?

tying the ears
of the garbage bag
together,
I notice the rabbit
on the patio

I go to meet him,
these hands brimming
with poems
running over and
spilling around my feet

M. Kei

July 6

rip the lid off
the box called
"today" and
spill it
everywhere

July 7

accidentally
scaring myself with
ghost stories,
it's a long while
before I can sleep

M. Kei

July 10

needing
to shave with
my glasses on,
this too is
middle age

mourning doves
perched on power lines—
how do they escape
the electric shock
of knowing all?

he came by train,
his wheelchair
the first part of him
to appear
on the platform

what is the name
for that exact shade
of gray
hanging over my head
this morning?

ring marks
in the swollen knuckle,
a little more
middle age
this morning

how to explain
to a son
just sixteen
the miracle of this
green morning?

the willow tree
tumbled but not toppled,
nearly leafless,
but its roots still cling
to a rocky shore

M. Kei

an afternoon
as ordinary as
seagulls,
but two lovers
pose forever

I'd like to
pour today's heat
into bottles
and keep it for
mid-winter

a migraine,
a pill,
a sweltering afternoon,
clouds without rain,
days without love

that tree
with the wilted green leaves
as breathless
as this sleeper
on a July afternoon

July 12

I didn't like my job,
but I miss
having it—
these empty days
of withered leaves

cold dew on
wild black raspberries—
these are the dawns
that carry summer into
the winter of our years

M. Kei

July 15

poledancer,
tall ship style—
up the mast
in the bosun's chair
to reclaim the flag halyard

in the bosun's chair
above the shrouds,
a certain irony
in the naming of
spars and lines

no safety net
under the bowsprit—
just the chains,
the sea,
and duty

<u>July 16</u>

dreams
stuck to the pavement
like melted ice cream
 your words
 a gathering of flies

tucked into
the poetry journal:
 oil change coupon
 unemployment check
 very short grocery list

that blue sky
is so very far away,
no matter how
I try, I will
never reach it

M. Kei

July 17

my son does
a load of dishes,
then I do,
a pair of bachelors
waking up the moon

that dog can
run on water—
the joy of
chasing ducks
never caught

the waitress and I
compare broken fingers
while she makes
change for
my breakfast

July 20

wearing the
bones of earth,
I slip through
the shadows
of the day

a bridge of bones
carries the dreamrider
on his nightmare
through haunted woods
that look exactly like home

in a dream
if a coyote calls
answer
with another's
voice

M. Kei

July 24

even in this rain,
or perhaps
because of it,
my face
turns to the sea

Sabbath morning
going down to the sea
and raising the sail,
a white prayer
going up to the sky

cloudbow—
thin clouds
a prism
for the light
of many colors

crows arguing
in the summer heat;
limp trees
waiting for the storm
to break

autumn—
dark skies
illuminated by
the golden lamps
of trees

all evening long
the anxious and
repeated rattle
of the dowager
cardinal's song

six billion people
and still procreating;
you'd think with so
many choices,
I'd find one for me

M. Kei

a humid night,
the neighbors' windows
closed against
the songs of frogs and
dusk piled deep

July 27

thunder
stacked on top
of thunder—
the closet starts
to look inviting

as sudden
as it came,
it leaves,
a summer storm
full of tornado fear

that sound again—
the one that might
not be a train—
hidden within the
roar of thunder

M. Kei

at the window,
listening for tornados—
no sound but
the storm, the sirens,
and crying children

July 28

I don't want
to see cathedrals
in France,
not with the Chesapeake Bay
spread out before me

August

August 3

it wasn't
the sort of dream that
keeps a man alive,
but it kept him awake
all through the humid night

a broken bottle—
many reflections
refracted through
the fractures of
the reflections

under the flag
of heroes,
the charred ruins
of a girl
without sin

M. Kei

her veil of hair
screaming over
the bloody remains
of her youngest son
    my sister

the memory
comes unexpectedly,
I wonder
if there was very much
blood when he died

August 5

there's poetry
in everything, even
in the fear
at the top of
a swaying mast

M. Kei

August 8

being
like others
defeats
the purpose
of being

for years
this land has
worked me
until I am about
to disappear

somewhere
in the darkness
inside my heart
the lights of a distant city
are burning

August 10

in the end,
something called
"victory"
bleeding down
the wall

does the door
open in or out?
it all depends
which side
the cat is on

if you tilt
your satellite dish
just right,
you might hear
God calling

M. Kei

one bagpipe
in a mist-filled dawn—
that was the sound
of a lover's hopes
unfulfilled

August 13

I wanted to argue,
but the sandpaper of
his jaw
was more than my
lips could resist

M. Kei

August 14

these are the stars
that light our path,
these are the stars
that know our heart,
these are the stars of glory

this is not a moon
floating silver
in the sea,
this is not a night
as empty as me

I am not Basho,
I am that peasant
he found
digging potatoes
along the road

August 15

peel me
down to the bone,
to the white
bitter
heart of me

rain needles
piercing
right through
the green roof
of the world

tawny lilies—
there are other flowers,
but none that
give themselves
so freely to me

M. Kei

the landlord
doesn't see these nail holes
as I do:
hooks on which to hang
doors into other worlds

August 16

this town knows
the peace of Agamemnon,
murdered by those
who professed
to love it

a cowboy
as broken
as his horse,
the sunset far
from his reach

M. Kei

August 17

it was a schooner
that brought me to
this place,
met by old Dutch women
hawking lobsters

January, A Tanka Diary

August 19

there's a prison in your heart
and it keeps me captive,
dangling
between your breasts
on a silver chain

203

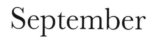

September

September 1

azure morning,
passing the crab boat
Aaramy,
working a line of
black pennants

M. Kei

September 2

bone-house
rocked on the dreaming tide,
oyster shell
and cockle bell
and all stations of the sun

the silent heat
of the autumn sun
binds the bone-house
in red ribbons
as night comes in

the windblown dream
of love—
tattered clouds of longing
through the seasons
of the night

September 15

Saturday morning—
a crow
picking at
the breadcrumbs of
my existence

M. Kei

September 20

pocket beach
full of sea wrack and
empty clam shells,
a driftwood tree
and a poet

a pocket beach
tucked amid boulders,
sea wrack and pebbles,
the voice of the waves
the only conversation

the bluffs
of Turkey Point
clouds
just beyond
my reach

empty
but still attached,
two clamshells
something like
a husband and wife

autumn hike
through a woody lane
both sides hugged
by stands of
wild peppermint

in the shade
of a walnut tree,
crows complaining
about the end
of summer

once perfectly black,
his coat now flecked
with white,
the cat keeps me
company tonight

September 29

someone's head
better than mine
propped up
for all eternity,
to be called "Art"

this is not Magritte's hat
this is not Magritte
this is not
this is
not

a few things called "art"
by Google:
a Nascar
a sleeping dog
a woman in a string bikini

hearing the news
he drowned
like
a butterfly
in a teacup

he points out
the place where they
burned the cross
and closed
the bridge to history

all around me
the golden brown
of autumn,
but the green, green waters
of Liberty Reservoir

a river full
of rising fogs—
Indian spirits
drifting beneath
the iron bridge

M. Kei

a gaunt white man
dredging the marina
with a small boat anchor,
bringing up lost lines
to scavenge their sinkers

Saturday night
the captain's baritone
on my voice mail—
I linger over it a little while
before returning his call

sleeping
with the window open,
autumn
a third quilt
upon my bed

I can't catch the cricket
and I won't kill it
every night
it sings autumn
under my bed

the rumble
of freight trains—
louder
after the leaves
have fallen

no God
but this day
glorious with the sky
the moon
and the sea

after dropping my son off,
the long legged heron
wading alone
in the storm water
catchment

the white coins
of clam shells
scattered on a beach;
the wealth of the world
beneath my feet

M. Kei

the toad is stubborn
I try to shoo him
to the shade of green shrubbery
but he won't go—
no one ever takes my advice

sneaking the cat
into her hospital room—
the "dumb animal"
understands
"goodbye forever"

October

October 1

Poole Island
a shore my foot
has never known,
yet it lies broad
across my dreams

I haven't had
a broken heart in years
it's an accomplishment
that leaves me
feeling a little sad

the October moon
a sliver in the blue sky
is all
I can give
to you

M. Kei

October 3

noticing the
female midshipman,
her crisp whites and bun—
that could have been
my daughter

October 4

outsailed
by a monarch butterfly
whose small wings
will carry him
all the way to Mexico

drowned island
beneath our keel,
if I reach down
will I find a hand
reaching up?

that island is
nothing but dredge spoil
torn from the channel's bottom,
but see its green temples
and blond beaches

M. Kei

I crave
a patch of green land
to belong to me
as I belong to it
this autumn day

I don't think
I'd be lonely on
an island
with nothing
but herons

October 10

this night
so big
not even
Bach
can fill it

the hawk spreads
her broad wings,
but I am clipped
and cannot
answer her call

a raft of seaweed
has drifted close to shore,
as if it too
needs a haven in
autumn's dying days

M. Kei

October 12

standing in
the clockshop,
waiting for 'now'
to happen
all at once

a vale of shadows—
then one ray of sun strikes
the green earth
and the woods are lit
with golden splendor

men of the house,
hung on the clothesline
fresh clean
boxer shorts for me,
small white briefs for my son

the cardinal
cocks her head
as if
this patch of dirt
meant something

M. Kei

October 13

"coffin bunk"—
the dead have better
accommodations
than this wooden hole
under the starboard deck

dinner begins
with a safety talk:
in the event of emergency,
pull the ceiling knobs
for life jackets

October 16

the World Tree
grows in this vacant lot,
ragged and vine-strangled
but green
and greener still

before dawn,
chasing the sun
out of the hills,
its great mirror
shimmering gold

M. Kei

October 17

a raft of waterfowl
vague
in the morning mist
the red disk of the sun
the only color

the muffled thump
of artillery as we pass
the proving ground,
fog, water, and dawn,
mute in the autumn morning

the rising sun
finally
strong enough
to warm my face
this autumn morning

off the Sassafras River
the Eagles sing,
"Take it easy"
crab boats
work their lines

the first range marker
the faintest trace
of Poole Island
low in the fog
behind it

work day on the Bay:
a barge
steaming south,
a crab boat
working her lines

late autumn—
a deadrise
steams home,
her roof loaded
with crab pots

M. Kei

slate waters
the eastern sky
full of grey clouds
a dark bar
of land in between

a work day
in autumn—
no pleasure boats
on these
cold waters

the captain
with his back
to the mast,
hat over his eyes,
napping

a world of darkness
water, sky, shore . . .
then the glint
of sun diamonds
on the water

a Bay without
any pleasure boats,
their skippers ashore
in comfortable quarters,
sipping hot cider

a pleasure boat
never knows the Bay
like an oysterboat does,
with winter looming
behind the horizon

rockinghorse swells—
the pony boat
bobs her head
as she canters
over the waves

meandering south
at the helm of
the *Martha Lewis*,
the number of pleasure boats
increases with the temperature

M. Kei

center span
of the Bay Bridge
all courses converge—
tugs, freighters,
skipjacks, powerboats

the deadrise
Shameless
zooms past with
her Virginia bow
in the air

Bay Bridge—
I've been under it
more times
than I've been
over it

Woodwind II
in full sail,
blue pennon
snapping in
the breeze

pleasure boats
on the Severn River
the last
monarch butterfly
of the season

the rusty red silhouette
of Bloody Point Light,
the white hull of a
deadrise skimming
past its base

Knapp Narrows:
on one side
million dollar yachts,
on the other
deadrises and derelict buyboats

M. Kei

October 18

5:30 am
a deadrise zips into the cove;
a waterman goes into
the corner store and
returns with a hot coffee

shore houses
still dark beneath
rose and amber clouds:
dawn over
Tilghman's Island

in the middle
of the Bay,
both shores
dark smudges
on the horizons

toilet paper
in short supply
aboard the boat—
I hold it
a little longer

Holland Island Bar Light
shrinking astern,
but Solomon's Lump Light
no nearer or brighter
this afternoon

the great expanse
of the Chesapeake Bay
empty
but for
one skipjack

"Southern Culture on the Skids"
blaring from the speakers,
the skipjack
plows the waters
of Kedges Strait

M. Kei

a beam sea
and the starboard deck
wet with spray,
indistinguishable from
the first drops of rain

October 19

Orion
has gone to sleep,
I rise
from a bed of mist
on Galen's Creek

the magic trick
of dawn:
a slim white sailboat
materializes
from the mist

my hand on the tiller
like Water Rat and Mole,
with no particular place to go
and no particular desire
to get there any time soon

M. Kei

no boat made
of plastic and aluminum
can ever equal the pleasure
of a log canoe
with a patched wooden hull

Crisfield's Old Island:
a chimney and brambles
all that's left
of a once thriving
fish processing plant

October 20

a fair day
in the offing,
mackerel clouds
and a mellow sea
in an autumn dawn

a hunting pelican
the brown and white
flash of wings
skimming low
over the water

off Janes Island
a pair of pelicans
skimming the water
faster than
our motor can push

M. Kei

cottonball clouds
piling up in the
northwestern sky,
sailboats heeling
with the gusts

waking from a nap
to sunshine and
Frank Sinatra singing,
"The Sunny Side
of the Street"

a fast tide running
under the drawbridge—
I miss the throw
and we drift
dangerously close

brown haze
on the western shore—
the smell
of a wildfire
drifting over the water

October 21

Tolchester Beach
the white sails
of pleasure boats
in Baltimore's smog
on a sunny afternoon

passing Poole Island
the first range light appears—
in the home stretch,
I long for a hot shower
in my own house

shabby autumn woods,
stripped
of their summer finery,
down to the bare bones
of winter

November

November 4

bomb threat
at the Wal-mart—
customers and clerks
shivering under
the autumn sky

M. Kei

November 10

one son dead,
the other shipped
to Afghanistan—
my sister's
long winter

tying up the boat,
stowing gear,
one bushel of oysters
to the marina owner
pays the dockage

November 12

baby physics—
proving for herself
that applesauce
always
falls down

M. Kei

November 14

kisses
like bruises
and the
dark shadow
of memory

November 16

I want to
eat some poems
my brain
is hungry
tonight

M. Kei

November 18

waking at
my accustomed hour,
a dream of rain
still damp on the bark
of autumn trees

watching tv
with my son,
explosions and
popular science
bring us closer

having lost
her keys,
my daughter
comes tapping
at my morning window

November 19

home from work
I find a freshly plucked chicken
in the refrigerator,
and know
my daughter was here

M. Kei

November 24

old boats
were once sapling trees,
and in between,
a keel was laid on
the bright green grass

November 29

I could
give you the stars
in winter,
if only you would
step outside

December

December 3

noon
the sun low
in the sky
the air sharp
as crystal

the path
that was once
shut up
by summer's green gates
is now open

warm, these woods,
on a winter's day
sunlight streaking
through swaying limbs
shorn of leaves

M. Kei

the brambles
pluck my sleeve,
"tread lightly,
stranger to this wild place,
for you are not alone"

the control point
with its ribbons
and soda cans,
meaning even less
under a hawk wind

visible
through the trees
a house trailer,
roof tarps flapping,
tires for weights

go deeper
into the woods
where moss
is still green
under the fallen leaves

the alleys
of the forest
narrow,
lined with brambles
and silence

this is the place
where the dead doe lay
last spring—
nothing left but
a huddle of broken bones

a little fur
surrounding empty
eye sockets,
the rest of her
picked clean

last spring
I walked this path
finding redemption
in the blooms,
but now, only wind

M. Kei

a bent willow
twisted in its youth,
a few shreds
of faded yellow leaves
dangling in the breeze

taking shelter
within the woods,
I find a burrow,
a few brown leaves
filling its mouth

you could never
walk this wood twice,
no matter
how many times
you tried it

the woods
that seemed impenetrable
in summer
are hollow in
December's wind

wind driven,
a brown bramble
catches my shoulder
and I sit on
last spring's stone

in spring
when all was lush,
I was a little afraid,
but now I linger
reluctant to leave

the dying wood
winter weak
past its autumn glory
plays a minor tune
few will hear

the last flicker
bursts into flight
at my approach—
a flash of yellow
and it's gone

M. Kei

the wood sorrel
is still green,
tiny strawberry-like leaves
small against
the winter ground

another stake
that calls itself
"control point"
the sound of garbage cans,
the barking of dogs

last year's
discarded Christmas trees
needles faded
at last to
the color of straw

I took
no watch or key,
no money or ID,
as I walked in
the winter wind

last spring
this hedge was
a heap of lilacs,
now collapsed bushes
catch windblown trash

the lamps
of autumn
are extinguished
leaving only the
thin brown of leaves

singing
Amazing Grace
by her open grave
a winter storm
filling the sky

M. Kei

December 4

my daughter
sings along with
J-pop
while writing a paper
about ESOL teaching

"mira"
he tells me
and I look,
Guatemala suddenly appearing
in the electronics department

the little boy
translating for his parents
can't be more than five:
his dignity as he
accepts the responsibility

dismayed
I am the center of
complaints:
I helped the customer
by speaking Spanish

Bay Country—
cold now
I will hike
the silence
to Turkey Point

dark
and darker still
as the hawk wind
blows through windows,
doors, and dreams

yellow flicker
come to these
cold woods—
show me that I will
not be alone this winter

M. Kei

as usual
the phone call
is a wrong number—
dunned for
someone else's bills

a few white flakes
spangle a brown landscape
  inside the apartment,
  a picture of a Yule log
  on the computer screen

December 11

witching hour
in the Wal-mart parking lot:
rounding up carts
mist haloes
around the lights

December 14

a tree
full of fog,
sealing
the world
in a silent tomb

Midnight—
no hurry,
just a poet
driving home
after work

December 16

"body by Martha"
hauling her mainsail
lifting the boom
bowstringing the bowlines
raising the pushboat

female cardinals
as brown as the rain,
my autistic son
playing by himself
in the other room

December afternoon—
the white flash
of a squirrel's belly
leaping through
rain dark trees

M. Kei

the claws
of a hawk wind tear
the yellow moon
from the clouds
and drop it in the sea

December 31

last night
of the year—
another
set of hopes
abandoned

Credits

Periodicals & Websites
American Tanka. United States.
Atlas Poetica : A Journal of Poetry of Place in Contemporary Tanka.
   United States.
Blogging Along Tobacco Road. United States.
bottle rockets. United States.
Chrysanthemum. Austria.
Dragonfly Archives. 2009. <http://
   dragonflycollection.blogspot.com>
Eucalypt. Australia.
Gusts : Contemporary Tanka. Canada.
Haiku : Revistă de interferențe culturale româno-japoneze. Romania.
Ink, Sweat, and Tears. United States.
Kokako. New Zealand.
Lynx, a journal for linking poets. United States.
Magnapoets. Canada
Mariposa. United States.
Modern English Tanka. United States.
moonset : the newspaper. United States.
Notes from the Gean : A Journal of Japanese Short Forms. United
   States.
Prune Juice : A Journal of Kyoka and Senryu. United States.
Red Lights. United States.
Ribbons : The Journal of the Tanka Society of America. United
   States.
Simply Haiku. Philippines.
Skylark. United Kingdom.
Twitter.
White Lotus. United States.
Wisteria : A Journal for Haiku, Tanka, and Senryu. United States.

Anthologies
Antonovic, Aurora, ed. *Butterfly Away : Magnapoets Anthology
   Series 3.* Tecumseh, ONT: Magnaprint, 2011.
Antonovic, Aurora, ed. *Many Windows : Magnapoets Anthology
   Series 4.* Tecumseh, ONT: Magnaprint, 2011.
Aurora Antonovic, ed. *One Hundred Droplets : Magnapoets
   Anthology Series 1.* Tecumseh, ONT: Magnaprint, 2009.
Antonovic, Aurora, ed. *While the Light Holds : Magnapoets
   Anthology Series 2.* Tecumseh, ONT: Magnaprint, 2009.
George, Beverley, ed. *Tea Towel Tanka : Responses by poets in 2008
   to the art of Ōtagaki Rengetsu 1791 - 1875.* Pearl Beach, AUS:
   A Eucalypt Publication, 2008.
Kei, M. ed., *Catzilla! Tanka, Kyoka, and Gogyoshi About Cats.*
   Perryville, MD: Keibooks, 2010.

Kei, M., Sanford Goldstein, Pamela A. Babusci, Bob Lucky, Patricia Primes, & Kala Ramesh, eds. *Take Five : Best Contemporary Tanka*. Baltimore, MD: MET Press, 2009.
Mankh, ed. *2010 Calendar : Haiku Calendar*. Selden, NY: Allbooks, 2009.
McClintock, Michael, ed. *Streetlights : Urban Poetry*. Baltimore, MD: MET, 2009.
Rotella, Alexis & Denis M. Garrison, eds. *Ash Moon : Tanka on Aging*. Baltimore, MD: MET Press, 2008.
San Francisco Haiku Poets Tanka Contest. 2008.
Tanka Splendor Award. Gualala, CA: AHA Poetry. 2008.
Wilkinson, Liam, ed. *Nocturne*. York, UK: 3Lights Gallery, April - July, 2008. <http://threelightsgallery.com>
Wilkinson, Liam, ed. *Snow Days*. York, UK: 3Lights Gallery, January - March, 2009. <http://threelightsgallery.com>
Wilkinson, Liam, ed. *The Way Back Home*. York, UK: 3Lights Gallery. October - December 2008. <http://threelightsgallery.com>
Williams, Rodney, ed. *Snipe Rising from a Marsh*. Perryville, MD: Keibooks, 2012. <http://AtlasPoetica.org>

Collections
Kei, M. *Autumn Water : An Exhibition of Tanka*. Amy Kehring & Dale Johnson, photographers. Yorkshire, UK: 3Lights Haiku Gallery, October - December. <http://www.geocities.com/threelightsgallery/>
—*Bridge of Bones : A Tiny Tanka Chapbook*. Perryville, MD: Keibooks, 2007; *Bridge of Bones*. Pittsburgh, PA: Lilliput Review, 2008.
—*The Heart of a Sailor*. World Class Poetry. 2009. <http://www.world-class-poetry.com/poetry-toolbar.html>
—*Kujaku Poetry & Ships*. 2007. <http://kujakupoet.blogspot.com/>
—*Love Letters : Homoerotic Tanka of Love and Friendship*. York, UK: 3Lights Gallery, July 1 - September 30, 2008. <http://threelightsgallery.com>
—*Tangerine : A Tiny Tanka Chapbook*. Perryville, MD: Keibooks, 2007.

Publications by Keibooks

M. Kei's Poetry Collections

January, A Tanka Diary—New!

Slow Motion : The Log of a Chesapeake Bay Skipjack
tanka and short forms

Heron Sea : Short Poems of the Chesapeake Bay
tanka and short forms

Edited by M. Kei

*Fire Pearls : Short Masterpieces of the Human Heart (V. 1
& 2)*

Take Five : Best Contemporary Tanka (Vol. 4)

Catzilla! Tanka, Kyoka, and Gyogoshi about Cats

*Atlas Poetica : A Journal of Poetry of Place in
Contemporary Tanka*

Joy McCall, *circling smoke, scattered bones*—New!

M. Kei's Novels
in print and ebook

Pirates of the Narrow Seas 1 : The Sallee Rovers
Pirates of the Narrow Seas 2 : Men of Honor
Pirates of the Narrow Seas 3 : Iron Men
Pirates of the Narrow Seas 4 : Heart of Oak
*Man in the Crescent Moon : A Pirates of the Narrow Seas
Adventure*—New!
The Sea Leopard : A Pirates of the Narrow Seas Adventure
—Forthcoming, Summer, 2014

Fire Dragon

Made in the USA
Lexington, KY
22 November 2013